Squam Fever

SQUAM FEVER

poems Page P. Coulter
photographs Dale Lary

TOP OF THE WORLD PRESS · 2014

To Frances and Maxwell O. Phelps

who made Squam possible for us.

ACKNOWLEDGMENTS

"Mrs. Butterworth" *Embers*
"Reason" *Comstock Review*

www.pagecoulter.net
Photographs © 2014 Dale Lary

ISBN 978-0-9815929-9-2

Contents

Questions of Quiet

Splash

Splash!
into the lake.

Oh the spirited splendor
of a common splash.

It's there to spread happiness
and you can feel it
sweeping over you,
your body, your nerves,
your whole vacation.

The *splash*
of the canoe
as it enters the lake
from the ramp,
the *splash*
of loons, landing in front
of your cabin,
the *splash*
of sunset across your cove.

A splash has no shape,
making it hard to assemble.
It's therefore important
to catch it mid-air.

SQUAM FEVER

Nothing better than to slip naked into Squam
mornings when the lake itself is asleep
and above you a kingfisher is chattering,
watching for its breakfast catch
as you splash out to where the sun
shimmies over a mountain's peak.

No one is awake yet to peek
at you swimming alone in Squam,
enjoying the first glimmers of sun.
Let them sleep, let them sleep,
you intone to yourself as you catch
a glimpse of the tufted bird chattering

just as you notice your own teeth chattering
from the cold sting of water at the peak
of the morning's chill, aimed to catch
your breath, making you feel a wintry Squam
where earth, trees, and water sleep,
where a cold veil is dropped over the sun.

Back in the forties, father and son
would sneak out to go fishing, chattering
away, having wrestled out of sleep
from their beds, and now taking a peek
at lunch packed for the day on Squam
by moms, looking forward to their catch.

No cabins could be seen in this sleep-
imbued moment, but you might catch
the clanging bells of camps, nestled under peaks,
competing with the wakening sun,
or you might float among loons, chattering
not far from their nests on the edges of Squam.

Mornings when I peek at the sun
and catch the birds' chattering,
I rise from sleep, slide nakedly into Squam.

Yard Island

Not to own
but thoroughly enjoy

mornings early
before the guard
arrives

and to skinny dip
eat hastily-packed
ice coffee, bagels, even jam

to lie in the sand
of this glorious oasis
ours for the hour

Why We Never Went to Church on Church Island

Water, trees, landing rocks,
the birch bark cross, and
only my brother and me

bobbing along the whitecaps
sailing our catboat
along Church Island's shore

on other days than Sunday
when no motorboats and visitors
were assembled there.

Docks Made of Wood

Some docks bounce
cheerfully up and down
in waves.
Others don't.
But all
will bear the grief
I fear
of degenerative disease.

EAGLE WATCH

Just beyond *Yard Isles* on *Little Loon*
as a tired sun splays out across the lake
four eagle eyes catch my glance
from a nest built of mud and sticks
high up in a tree.

I ship my paddle,
glide silently under the stare.

Two fledglings, their soft down
turning to pinfeathers now,
hop and flap to the edge of the nest.

Across the slipping sun,
the male swoops down
with his catch, which he gives
to his mate, conveying a speechless
nudge of good will,
then spreads
his giant wings in flight.

A familial unity prevails.
For she is now feeding tidbits
into her youngsters' beaks.

As I watch from below,
I want to call out,
Please, weep for us, and all that closes around us into night.

The chicks re-arrange themselves
under their mother's wings.
I paddle home, as a wild aloneness
settles over Squam.

Big Loon

I feel the spine of the kayak
as it skims across the surface of Squam
mornings when the sun is creeping unseen
up the back side of Red Hill.

This is how I'd like my life to be:
sugar in the raw, flour unbleached,
the natural breadcrumbs of life.

My kayak points like a compass
to Big Loon, passing Little Loon
where eaglets are munching
their father's catch, and the pines
wink at the water's edge.

Flat rocks lead into Big Loon,
clear water lapping it,
inviting you to slide in.
It's all about today,
and how things want to be.

And when I beach the kayak
just as the sun rolls over Red Hill
the world wraps around me
in a perfect swirl.

Beyond our Sight and Understanding

Golden retrievers
sit on the end of every dock
waiting to converse with you
when you glide by in your canoe.

Tails wagging, they talk to you about
wonders they observe:
the way the moon waxes and wanes
like an old woman who never dies,
how the lake harbors unseen Indians
paddling by in birch canoes,
how the lake is weeping tears
of wear and distress.

They tell you this
in a language hard to understand,
but you nod,
and sometimes give them a pat
before you paddle on.

Squam Sunset

Sun going down, my father shouts,
and we all drop
what we are doing,
run to the porch
to watch the sun slide down
behind the mountains.

Who can say how many
have watched that sun
roll over to its other semi-sphere?
What I'm sure of is this:
we watched it every clear night
we were at Squam.
It was our inheritance.

My Mountain

My mountain hears what I have to say
It watches over me when I am sad

When I am happy it leads me to its highest peak
so we can celebrate together

Where have you been? it asks
I place a stone on its summit cairn

My mountain cares for me
It's all right to die: see the cowslips

and violets nodding by the stream? They come back every year
My mountain is naïve but age has given it wisdom

My mountain says, *It's better to follow a trail through the woods*
than to walk on tar

If you need friends, listen for the birds I've nested in my side for you
They are the truth of friends

Take off your shoes, so I can massage your feet
on my mossy rocks

My mountain lags behind when it rains
to play with the mist

My mountain meets with its friends to talk things over
Sometimes it takes a century

My mountain is wearing down. *Ten thousand years ago*, it sighs,
I was tall enough to block out your sun

When my mountain is sad, I tell it the story of Old Man, how he
is the one who made mountains, animals, trees and birds

Where is he now? it asks, and I tell it. Old Man walks every day
on his trails pointing to what he has made: he made the fox

that hides in your brambles; he made the blue jay, redpoll, and
goldfinch; he made wintergreen, star flower, and partridge berry

He made it all
Old Man is stooped and proud

He walks with a stick he found in the forest
My mountain is proud

Watches over and cares for me
I place a stone on its summit cairn

Not enough to sleep
in a rickety cabin
your father fiddled with
over the years, and where
your mother made
blueberry pies, where
beds were made up
with heavy cotton
coverlets.

We preferred to sleep
in tents next to the lapping lake
where mosquitoes zizzed
and loons made light the dark
with a-loo-loo-loo-ing tunes.

We toasted marshmallows
under the pines
in a makeshift fireplace of stones,
told stories, argued, laughed.
We took off our clothes, and dipped
into the chilling water,
trying not to wake the lady across the cove,
whose binoculars, we feared,
could see through night.

At last we'd zip open the tent,
snuggle into our sleeping bags,
refreshed and ready
for whatever dreams might visit us.

HAND PUMP AT MY AUNT'S COTTAGE

Rusted and cheerful
equipped to deliver
from under its well house

with two old tin cups
beside it
hanging from nails.

I think it's
still there.

A few hearty pulls
(how we fought for turns)
then whoosh!
Out water sloshes
from the spout

so virgin
so chill
so delicious.

BEACH SESTINA

Brilliant heat at the swimming beach;
bikini-clads stretch out their legs
boys play catch, girls shiver at the edge
mothers chat in chairs
watching toddlers splash.
Nothing disturbs this scene.

But wait; something only seen
to be believed waddles across the beach.
Toddlers stop their play mid-splash
as a mother mink on stubby legs
and with a long, thick tail, walks around the chairs
right up to the water's edge.

Mothers look up, aghast, nerves on edge
to watch this strange unfolding scene
then leap from their chairs
step quickly across the beach
to see five more with wobbly legs
come out from the rocks in a splash.

Most mothers are easy, with a splash
of occasional rigor, but now at the water's edge
with their own babies' chubby legs
maneuvering through this watery scene
and, with the entire nature of the beach
changed, they abandon their chairs

to protect their young, causing the chairs
to collapse and lie askew in the splash
of this moment at the lakeside beach.
The mother mink, meanwhile, nudges the edge
of the rocky outcrop, where the babies were seen
and pushes all five of them, all legs,

across in front of the toddlers' tottering legs,
past teens, wet tennis balls mid-air, and folded chairs.
She ignores this panic-stricken scene
as her babies wriggle and squiggle and splash
to the opposite edge
and more rock caves far across the beach.

Calm returns to the beach, and children on barefoot legs
run happily to the edge while mothers, back in chairs,
watch them splash like mink in this once-again summery scene.

26

HOLDERNESS

is where you go in your boat
for gas, ice cream cones
or Band-Aids and milk.

You tie up
at Squam Boats
then dash up the wooden steps

to do your errands quickly
before the tanks are filled
and your dog leaps off the boat

because you are the love of her life.
She sits at the bow of the boat
hoping not to be left behind

forever. Where would she go?
Who would feed her chunks of liver and beef?
Who would let her jump off the dock

to chase ducks she can't catch,
though it's fun to try? Who would
offer her handfuls of love on the porch?

But you return, motor under the bridge,
down the canal lined with nesting ducks,
then join an orchestra of wind,

water skiers and sailboats out across the lake.

Loons Wishing the Motor Boats Would Vanish

The best way to get to
where you are going
is by kayak
or canoe
loo-oo-hoo-aloo

..
29
..

POOH CORNER

They took down the house my father built.
Can you believe it?
Even the chimney with a granite stocking for a keystone.
Our summer camp on the lake.

The sleeping house big enough for two built-in beds and a
bedside lamp, with window boxes filled with asters.
The built-on addition called Wolery with a tiny trap door
big enough for a child or Very Small Bear to creep through.

And Sanders, a plywood cave under the house
with two beds and wooden life-size figures on the wall.
Christopher Robin, Pooh, Piglet, Eeyore.
All were there. Made from old leftover boards.

Tore it down.
My brother sold it.
So they razed it. They had to.
"The house wasn't big enough," the new owner said,
"for a family of four."

The picture window framing Bean Cove, the living room, the porch
where watching the sun set was a family ritual.
The game corner: Chutes and Ladders, Scrabble, Monopoly.
The wood box window seat against the fireplace.

The perch and bass forms cut from paper bags and tacked to the wall.
The giant wooden spoon and fork some guest left as a gift,
hanging over the kitchen pass-through.
Gramma's watercolor of a tree framed in birch.

Gone.

Vacations we all crowded in. Cousins. Friends.
There was always room for one more.
Sometimes a tent by the rocky shore where the bees hung out.
Or a make-shift cot on the porch. However many it took to make hilarity
and swimming from the dock more fun. We'd hardly notice when night crept
in through the open windows, carrying with it bats, the call of owls, crumb-
seeking mice, and the endless lapping of the lake against the rocks.

They took our cabin down to the ground.
"The kitchen," the new owner said, "was too small for a family who
loves to cook."

The pine needle terrace surrounded by a wall built from all the flat rocks
my father could find in the nearby woods.
The yellow linoleum floor in the kitchen where I once spilled a whole
blueberry pie then scooped it up to serve.

Taken away to the dump in a truck.

Nothing remains of the camp my mother and father built and loved and
brought us to year after year until late in their nineties when they died.
Nothing.
Except the trophy award-winning architect-designed
Adirondack house in its place.

"The powder room backsplash tiles," a magazine article said,
"are decorated with pine cones and pine boughs. And on the walls,
Ralph Lauren Natural paint."

Local Inhabitants

Clouds Over Squam Mountain Range

What wish could hold a mountain range
  whistling clouds across your face
    like flapping laundered things?

What kind of day would hurl them
  dark as rituals
    across the lake?

The wish I had was like a deep cave
  in your side.
    I watched it come
      then disappear.

I know enough
  not to shut my eyes
    to let the wind
      tell everyone's wish but yours.

At night clouds go behind you
  like a laundry woman done in,
    loose waves of gray
      down her back.

Old Man Stomps out of his Cave

Earth was Old Man's zone.
He noticed flowers,
birds, trees and stones; he named
them all from his bark canoe.

Greeks and Persians manned triremes
ramming, raping, wrestling foes,
their oars in perfect synchrony
as they sped impiously across wide seas.

Dragon-headed Viking ships
explored the outer world.
Mainstay of a pagan faith, they
carried the dead to afterlife.

Patrol torpedoes, PT boats
wrinkled World War Two,
planing oceans at twenty knots,
dubbed *devil boats* by Japanese.

Kayaking along a sphagnous bog,
I rue technology's success;
the Earth is vexed.

Old Man paddles home.

WHY NOT THE LADY'S SLIPPER

pink as Cinderella's cheeks
its composition, scent, and
luminous lure
so enticing
O to slip it on and be,
even as the world repeats its glorious myths,
a story told just once?

FROGS

Frogs, like thoughts,
lie in ambush
ready to jump
toward you
or away,
or sometimes
they simply
sit and croak.

Some are heavy
as dough,
some, green as
lily pads,
some, cheery as
a lollypop.

More often frogs
(as well as thoughts)
will appear
ready to pounce
then with a splash
be gone.

Research Scholar

Our resident squirrel,
tail arched and twitching,

each acorn, nut and seed
assessed for worth,

hoards windfalls
in caches
only he can find,

noses out his peers
with his savory
discoveries.

Is it done
for joy, for livelihood,
for recognition?

Will there be
a prize
some day

to honor him
in a language
never learned?

awarded such a fabulous tail displayed this cold sheer morning like a feather in a British lady's hat waving here then there to catch the perfect rays of the sun yes the body upside-down as it plunges head first into the sunflower seeds his gratis sustenance waving that bushy mass a flag so-to-speak

denoting courage in the face of lurking dog teeth gritting at the door that separates the two and yet he doesn't let the seeds pour in exactly he extracts them one by one and with his delicate tiny paws places them in his cheeks for a later chew all the time his perky ears flickering like miniature search-

lights for the least little flurry of hawk wings to make him scurry down the drainpipe to his hidden nest but two or three times a day he waddles slowly cautiously onto the deck like a country gentleman then whish! he's once more atop the feeder flinging his body down its length gripping it with all four paws

spilling seeds carelessly into his cheeks while the chickadees watch from trees and he feels entitled shameless too as he lets another seed drop into his mouth and why was he given that beautiful tail that almost makes you want to forgive him for taking from the meek to serve his own outrageous needs.

REDPOLLS

If I could be a bird
I'd choose the redpoll

join a flock
point my red spot north
and fly across the arctic plains

even as icebergs
gave themselves over
to global floods

and even as the last guitars
sank into the rising sea.

I'd capture some
lingering notes
attach them to
a singular song
for my mate.

We'd have all the time
in the universe
to sing to each other

no one to hear
but us.

..
41
..

Hairy Woodpecker

No ordinary apparition
can stun the atmosphere in such a way,
its plumage, red-capped, black and white,
declaring its wish to be seen.

And who has not heard it strike a hollow branch:
    Don't fritter fritter fritter,
      make life simpler simpler simpler still
        yet not monotonous monotonous, no
          not monotonous.

Yes, how we yearn for that simplicity.

Then, just like that, it soars aloft
a feathery flurry of flickering flight

TICKS

O hardy ticks
your season's here.
Upon dogs' backs
you'll soon appear.

Are ticks bad pests
or pests bad ticks?
Can ticks be tocked
or tocks be ticked?

They're like a teen
who can't be tamed
who snubs the rules
then won't be blamed.

It's in their blood
to counteract
this boring world
that made them fact.

A bite or two
to show who's who
and ever at
expense of you.

44

NOTHING IS HAPPENING BELOW MY DECK

But wait . . .

Over there, grasses
and Indian paintbrush waving,

and lupine ravaging the field like a wolf,
spreading its seeds from patch to patch.

Mourning doves intone laments:
a-loodle loo loo loo, a-loodle loo loo loo.
The pond is morning-still, peepers sleep.

A chipmunk peeks from the woodpile:
Is everything all clear?

Sapphire swallows swoop
in jagged lines through the air.

Everything else moves barely perceptibly,
as if something
or nothing might happen.

Even stalks of lupine,
purple and self-important, nod.

Everything is clear,
nor would I have it otherwise.

ALMOST SPRING

Underneath lies grief
in sodden leaves
asleep. I keep

it there. Like
herbal tea
I let it steep.

Yet now I see
ground cedar
peep above

thin gleams of
melting snow.
Hello, its heap

of tendrils calls
from out of
wintry sleep

*sleep of dreams, fall asleep, sleep-in, sleeping pills, sleeping bags,
sleeping cars, sleeplessness, asleep at the switch, asleep to the needs,
legs asleep, sleepy, sleep disorders, stages of sleep, sleep deprivation,
sleep band, sleep-over, sleep-wear, sleep walk, sleepy head, sleeping
sickness, sleep of your life.*

Like herbal tea
I let it steep.

Questions of Quiet

Summer Climb

My father made me understand
the woodpecker's need to strike
his beak against wild oaks. That
day I followed close behind him
up Mount Wonalancet, stopping
for views, or breath, or something
silent underneath tall pines. We
knew what we had left behind,
and only the touch of air against
our skin stirred our senses.

He told me how his brother once
chased him with an ax
all across Petit Manan, angry
that he'd drunk the ginger ale
that was for lunch. Was some
of that devil in me, I asked,
that made Mother cry? Our words
collusive ghosts, hung close to us
from outstretched boughs.

We put our shoes in his pack,
walked barefoot, hearing
soundlessness spread like
Indians up the trail behind.
Then the woodpecker struck
his taps, disengaging silence,
and we laughed outright,
letting Wonalancet fall
between our toes.

52

JACK

My brother Jack was a brat by two and a half.
Inside the pockets of his overalls he put

my mother's love, his marbles, and his jack-knife.
He used his model planes and crystal set

to show how wise he was. Outside sometimes
beside a stream, he picked sweet peas for Mom,

red columbine, and wild geraniums.
How sweet, she'd say. I hated his blue eyes.

He liked to tattle more than eat French toast.
Page is spitting from the roof, he'd say.

Then Mom, who took the bait without a thought,
would smack me while my brother watched with glee.

One day on a lake my brother tied himself
up tight inside a rubber raft. The wind

from round Mount Rattlesnake was stiff
enough to crack an egg. But Jack was bound

to tackle it as he had tackled *all* before.
His boat was flipped. I saw him go face down.

I let a moment pass. Then two. Three. Four.
Help, I screamed, *Help, it's Jack. He's fallen in.*

They rescued him and when he overcame the shock,
he barked, *Page flipped me from the dock.*

MRS. BUTTERWORTH

Mrs. Butterworth
came to my father for shots,
called, *Hello Pagie dear,*
was stopped at the mouth's edge
from trying my chocolates, by Mother,
whose look slides across time as a dune of sky.

I, being ten and careless on Squam,
could offer Mrs. Butterworth chocolate-
covered soap, swim naked
with my brothers,
build a boat with leftover boards,
be first to the top of Rattlesnake,
beg my father for stories.

Uncle Paul,
Mrs. Butterworth's husband,
invited us over to splatter paint
his kitchen floor,
taught me the call of the Great Blue Heron,
directed the bird call game in his barn.
Mrs. Butterworth didn't play.

Uncle Paul knew how Chocorua,
being chased by a white man, leaped
to his death from Chocorua rock,
how to make gum from tree sap,
how the cows got stuck in cow cave.
He and Mrs. Butterworth never had cocktails.
We hid the glasses whenever they came.

Uncle Paul once
took us on an all day trek
across Sandwich Range.
There was no trail.
When he got tired, we looked at tufts
of bear hair or glacial potholes, or wrote
our names on fungus.

We jumped off the dock
with all our clothes on
when we got back.
Being ten and careless, I spattered
my happiness all over Squam.

Dr. Unsworth

My mother taught us
to look people straight in the eye
whenever we shook hands,
something I really didn't want to do.
I did not want to tell Dr. Unsworth
how I did, or what grade
I was in at school.
So I dove into his fish-blue eyes,
swam around the iris, slid
down his watery cataracts.

Not that I knew anything
about eyes at that time.
All I knew
were the optic words
Dr. Unsworth spoke
one grunt at a time
at parties with my parents
and all their other
doctor friends and wives
before he would fall asleep
behind the couch.

He always drove their Pontiac hell-bent,
especially around *S* curves,
ignoring angry beeps,
as if he were a god.
I saw that in his eyes
whenever I shook his hand.

POPPY SEEDS

Summers we drove seven hours to Squam,
where my father taught us how to sail
by shoving us into our sailboat from the dock.
Lines whipped to free themselves from main and jib,

and us, while we shouted commands to each other that
only we could understand. His complete calm,
standing there on the dock, with his hands halfway
down his hips, watching us, invited us

to believe in ourselves. I can't think of a single word
he ever said that sounded professorial. If
we learned to sail, we did it ourselves, with only
his confidence swirling above us like a Ferris wheel.

Our lives were happy as poppy seeds.

DEVIL STICK

Then fancies flee away, I'll fear not what they say,
I'll labor night and day to be a pilgrim. — *John Bunyan*

At camp on Squam, one girl is called
to shake the Devil Stick all through
To be a Pilgrim's final verse.

The stick, a knobbly branch
of brightly painted wavy shapes,
worn smooth by campers' hands,
chases the Devil from our midst.

Doc Ann, our leader, says the Devil
laughs at girls who give up and lose.
Our skin, pinched from early morning swims,
ripples and jerks as the Devil makes second best

seem immoral.
Winters, home at last,
we eat wheat bread, do whatever is asked,
yet when I close my eyes, the Devil grins.

When at last I enter motherhood
I'm not surprised to feel the Devil's twinge,
icy as a lake, as it pries open
my eyes so that I may watch it

carry off my daughter, Susan.
But then, reviving Doc Ann's long-ago taunt,
I shake the Devil Stick
till Susan's dread disease subsides.

I watch the Devil disappear,
tail between its knees.

The Art of Finding a Religion

When asked to draw a picture of God
my brother, at five, drew a fisherman
fishing from his rowboat.

Summers, we'd watch this god and his friends
put-put into our cove
laughing, drinking beer,
casting again and again.

They were a religion unto themselves
and we could feel it fill the morning breeze,

move across the misty lake
to where we stood on the dock.
And when their poles were bent

from a mighty catch, we'd wave
and shout, even as these gods
took another sip of beer

then lifted their rods
to catch another pickerel or trout.

FLUTIST ON THE DOCK AT SQUAM
for Emilie

Sometimes strong-armed gods
inside this fluid mass hurl rocks
at mountain tops. Yet now,
they are calm, blowing breath
through her flute as she stands

on the dock late tonight, playing
to loons, unwritten storms,
and bullfish. Loving their mirror
image, the gods lie back,
rippling the waves, causing them

to lap the lichen-covered rocks
on shore. She plays a Bach sonata,
transforming the gods to dancing fish;
they, knowing good times, push bubbles
from their lips, waving their tails

in a rhythmic swish, and playing their
scales against surface moonlight.
They move in schools, as if
they were cadenzas, showing
their virtuosity. And they catch

her melodies that skim a film
of sound across the lake. Have they not
been told she plays the shadow that
attaches her to gods, to earth,
to wavy lines of water?

SQUAM NIGHT

You're not coming back.
For a year, I thought the pillow
on your side of the bed, was you,
only to be saddened
when I awoke.

Now I know it's true.
The garden is mine;
I'll have to deal with slugs
on tomato plants myself,
and your Sunday omelette
will sit in the egg box
unrealized.

Last night on Squam
your absence spoke
with a silent roar
surrounding the boat
as we ate our picnic
and watched two loons glide by
alone with your thoughts.

QUESTIONS OF QUIET

Wherever quiet goes
   paddling, winding,
      or flowing

through bogs, the marsh,
   the open lake
      now here
         now there

seeing—
   yes how *quiet* itself
      sees it all—

and whenever I
   reach out my hand
      to pull it in

it floats right through me
   carrying
      the whole earth's silent drum.

I feel its whim beside me
   paddling
      paddling.

REASON

in memory of Judy Streeter

Whenever the gods call out to the loons
and the loons reply across the still morning lake
and the sun squints pensively above them
and the trees shift, making lofts for their song,

It must be to soften a person's sorrow,
taking its steady-going stream across
the mountain range through clouds that
wind and cushion it like an accidental plaything.

It must be to settle the placement of change,
the way mist will rise balloon-like over the lake
making visible blue pickerel weed, swamp grass,
and the glazed broad faces of lily pads.

Or to let you feel, yet not quite understand,
the sadness that surrounds this body of
remembrance, wafting above you,
above this chill New England day,

inviting no answers, no just replies.

SANDWICH BEACH, OCTOBER

The resident loon and his mate have left
for the eastern shores of Maine.

Now rains blow in from the south,
patting down sand where

Wonalancet kneels to mourn the loss
of his father and all things lost to the sky.

He cups his hand for a drink, squinting at
the mountains across the lake.

If only they'd come back, he reflects,
even as maples on shore blur to the feast

of pelting rain and mist. He reaches
through brambles for a handful of

thimbleberries, wrestling with his pain.
Be kind, The Great Spirit whispers in his ear,

Be kind to all, as your father, Passaconaway, was.
These words we hear in the breaking waves.

DEPARTURES

At breakfast I notice the birds are gone,
no longer speckling the sloping roof
no longer waiting turns at the feeder.

What do I know of a redpoll's nature?
Is some neighbor serving tastier fare,
better cover? Are they off to colder climes?

I solve the daily crossword, clean the fridge,
seek out a sunny chair,
recall the *tp tp tp* of chattering birds.

Remembrance trumps departure, I say to myself,

remembering the fleeing flock
as words reverberating
close and calm.

Local Weather

The mountains have returned from the mist.
As far east as Maine, the mist is retreating

below hovering rain-laden clouds. High winds
and cold air are forecast to arrive from the west.

In the south, your gravestone stands
in front of a time-worn stone wall,

calm as a lone sheep grazing
or the deep breath of loss.

The Moment the Mountains Drop out of Sight

The mountains cannot be seen
behind the near trees.

It's like setting out seines
in a murky sea

or seeing to it that dreams become
what they leave behind.

I am here in this mist-laden moment
making promises to myself

that all will be well, that what is
lost from view will be retrieved.

LABOR DAY

It's Labor Day and the mice
look forward to time alone
in summer camps.

Windows are boarded shut,
old sheets spread over
moth-eaten coverlets, chairs
and couches with sprung springs.

Un-canned food is packed away
in cars returning to Boston, Philadelphia,
or other towns far away from the lake.

Darkness prevails inside, and you feel
a restless thumping inside your heart
as you bid good-bye to the cabin for a year.

The boats are pulled up
and stored under the house,
the flag on the end of your dock, folded
and stored in a moth-balled box.

You put the key you never use
into the lock at the kitchen door,
give it a final twist,

Good-bye, Squam,
and may the mice be content
till next year.